Cello Time Spri[nters]

Piano accompaniment book

Kathy and David Blackwell

Contents

MUSIC DEPARTMENT

OXFORD
UNIVERSITY PRESS

1. Carnival jig

KB & DB

Printed in Great Britain

OXFORD UNIVERSITY PRESS, MUSIC DEPARTMENT, GREAT CLARENDON STREET, OXFORD OX2 6DP

2. Spic and span

KB & DB

4. Stop—start

KB & DB

5. River song

KB & DB

6. Overture

A Baroque celebration

KB & DB

7. Going fourth

KB & DB

With thanks to Tom Morter for this idea.

8. City streets

KB & DB

10. Metro line

KB & DB

With attitude

11. Falling leaves

KB & DB

12. Holiday in Havana

KB & DB

14. Night shift

KB & DB

15. Le Tambourin

J. Ph. Rameau (1683–1764)
(adapted)

A tambourin was a lively 18th-century French dance, often accompanied by pipe and tabor.

17. Beyond the horizon

KB & DB

18. Sto me

Bulgarian trad.

With energy

20. Andante

Edward Elgar (1857–1934)

21. Joker in the pack

KB & DB

23. Comin' home

KB & DB

21

24. Sprint finish

KB & DB

25. In memory

(for Eileen)

KB & DB

26. Some day

KB & DB

26

27. Wild West

KB & DB

28. Je pense à toi

(for Clare)

KB & DB

29. Russian wedding

KB & DB

30. Two Songs from Dichterliebe

1. The lovely month of May

Robert Schumann (1810–56)
(adapted)

The repeat is written out in the cello part.

33

2. The rose and the lily

Allegro

31. Latin nights

Tango

KB & DB

Con fuoco

The last repeat is written out in the cello part.

32. 4th dimension

KB & DB

Funky

33. Fifth Avenue

(for Iain)

KB & DB